CHANGED *without* REGRETS

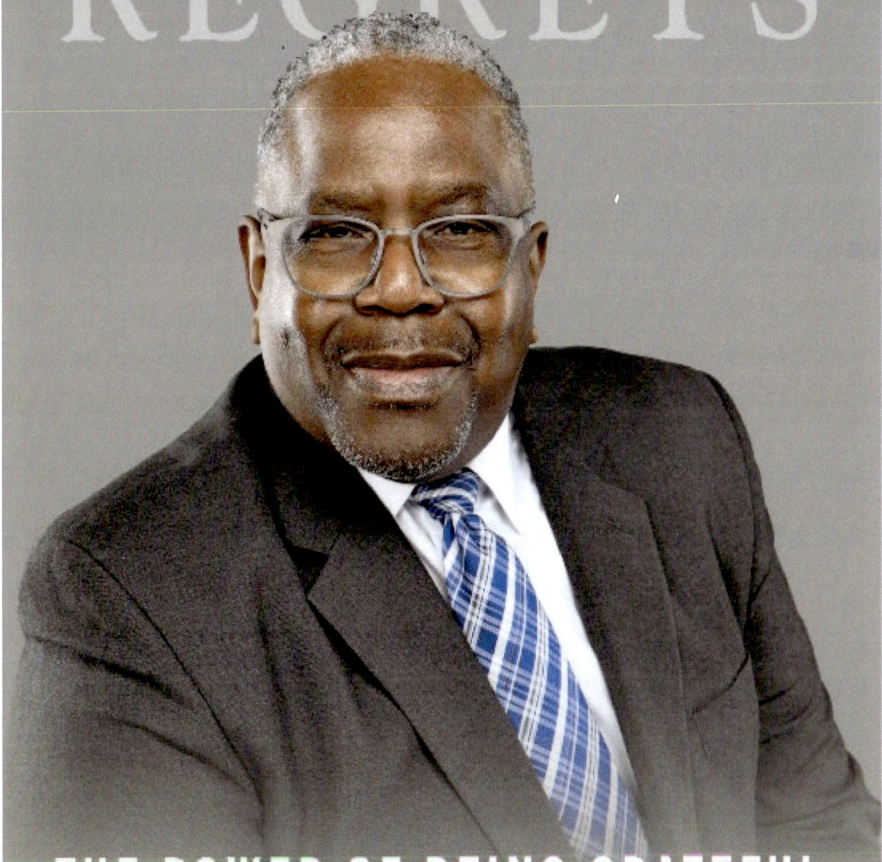

THE POWER OF BEING GRATEFUL

DR. CLYDE & WANDA FLOYD

ISBN- 979-8-9879298-4-1
Book cover design by Untouchable Designz and Consulting
Printed and bound in the United States of America

It Couldn't Be Done

BY: EDGAR ALBERT GUEST

Somebody said that it couldn't be done

But he with a chuckle replied

That "maybe it couldn't," but he would be one

Who wouldn't say so till he'd tried

So he buckled right in with the trace of a grin

On his face, if he worried he hid it.

He started to sing as he tackled the thing

That couldn't be done, and he did it!

There are thousands to tell you it cannot be done,

There are thousands to prophesy failure,

There are thousands to point out to you one by one,

The dangers that wait to assail you,

But just buckle in with a bit of a grin,

Just take off your coat and go to it;

Just start in to sing as you tackle the thing

That "cannot be done" and you'll do it.

TABLE OF CONTENTS

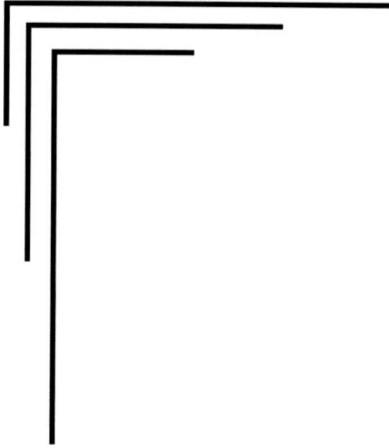

"I have fought the good fight, I have finished my course, I have kept the faith."

2 Timothy 4:7

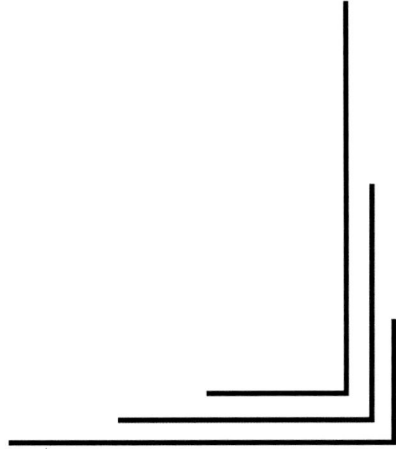

DEDICATION

This book is dedicated to my Pastor and mentor, the late Bishop Joseph P. Cooper Sr. He instructed me in the ways of living a holy and pleasing life to God. He exhibited a genuine love for God, his family, and the church. He was truly a pioneer for the 21st-century move of God. 2 Timothy 4:7 states, *"I have fought a good fight, I have finished my course, I have kept the faith……."* and at the age of 93, the Lord called him home to receive his reward.

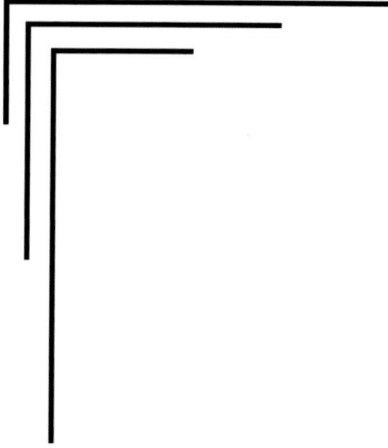

"For the prophecy came not in old times by the will of man; but holy men of God spoke as they were moved by the Holy Ghost."

2 Peter 1:21

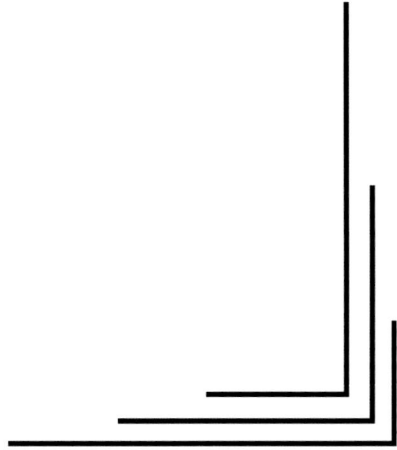

INTRODUCTION

This is my story. I am not a writer or author, but I am a believer in the miraculous power of God. I was inspired to write this book by the moving of the Holy Spirit that people's lives should be changed by the power of God. 2 Peter 1:21 quotes, *"For the prophecy came not in old times by the will of man: but holy men of God spoke as they were moved by the Holy Ghost."* The truth of the matter is that I was a sinner and backslider that did not deserve to live but because of the cross, Jesus gave me another chance. My mission is to spread the good news of Jesus Christ wherever I go so that souls will be set free and delivered by the power of God.

The world will entice you creating a false sense of hopelessness and with technology on the rise and the economy failing, whom can you trust? The answer is found in St. John 3:16, *"For God so love the world that he gave his only begotten son that whosoever believeth in him should not perish but have everlasting life."* Therefore, this book is dedicated to the lost and found.

If you have the ambition to serve and become a disciple today while anticipating tomorrow's possibilities, then Jesus Christ is just what you need to unlock your future. We must ask ourselves this question. Have I ever been set up to fail? If the answer is yes, today I challenge you to give all of your problems to God and trust him to take your dreams and make them into a reality.

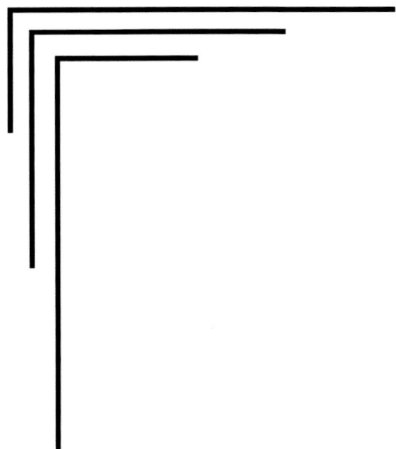

"God is our refuge and strength, a very present help in trouble."

Psalm 46:1

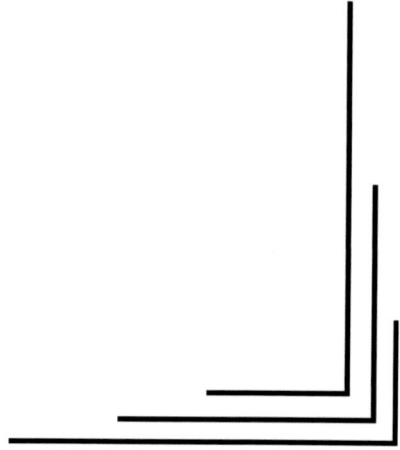

Chapter One

Upper King Road

My journey back home began with a visit one Sunday morning to my mother's house with no recollection of how I arrived there. Did I walk or did I get dropped off? I don't know. Only God knows!! I believe when God is calling you there is a point of reference just as when He called Moses, Paul, and Abraham for service. Little did I know; THIS day my life would change forever. After eating and chatting, I was on my way with no destination in mind and a bag in my hand feeling hopeless and alone. As bad asked it looked, God had a plan for my life. As I continued to walk up Upper King Road, I recognized a little blue truck in the distance. Lo and behold, it was my brother coming toward me. Psalm 46:1, states: *"God is our refuge and strength a very present help in the time of trouble...."* I was at the right place at the right time. He had just left church and was on his way to visit our mother. We talked very briefly and surprisingly he asked me if I would like to attend the afternoon service. I tried making excuses but finally gave in.

With no job, no money, and no place to live he carried me to a nearby clothing store to purchase something to wear that afternoon. God will supply your needs. In November of 1991, God restored me back into fellowship not just to the church but with my savior and my Lord Jesus Christ. II Corinthians 5:17 states, *"Therefore, if any man be in Christ, he is a new creature; old things are passed away behold all things become new."* At this time, the church was in the process of building a new sanctuary and I became instrumental in the finishing work with Bishop Cooper. I backslid and left the church to do my own thing however, God flipped the script, and what was meant for evil God turned it around for my good.

If you have any doubt that God is not speaking, He will make himself known. There was a time that I was sitting in a service and was wearing a red sweater. As the preacher was preaching, I asked the

Lord, is it my time? Right then the Lord gave the preacher a word just for me. He said, "You in the red sweater, are you saved?" The Bible says the day you hear his voice harden not your heart. That day I believed that God was calling my name. When you ask God a question, He will give you an answer.

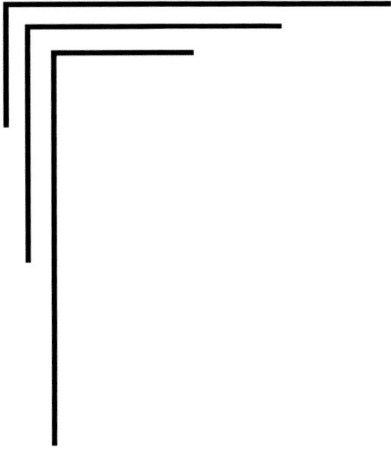

"Greater is he that is in me than he that is in the world."

1 John 4:4

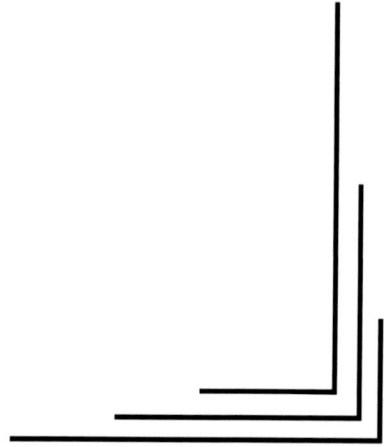

Chapter Two

Relationship Restored

At this time in my life, my wife and I had been married for approximately eight years, but we were not together. She was attending one church, and I was attending my foundational church. One Saturday night, there was a platform service, and I was one of the speakers. I invited her to come. Although she seemed very apprehensive, she came. Not knowing what to expect, I simply prayed for the best outcome. After the service, we went back to my mother's house, and she informed me and my mother that the Lord spoke to her during the service and let her know that this was

where she belonged. The next morning, she called Bishop Cooper and let him know what took place at the service that night. He instructed her what to do and she complied. This was the start of the restoration process.

At this time, I was still unemployed, and my wife was only working part-time but we believed that God had a plan for our lives. In spite of our current condition, we were faithful to the ministry and were learning to lean and depend on God. As a result, God began to show us His miraculous powers. With only one income, He allowed us to move into an apartment together. The landlord stated that she didn't know why she was approving us, but she did, and we never missed a payment. God can do exceedingly and abundantly above what we think or ask. The enemy was still on his job; trying to cause confusion and dissension between us but, 1 John 4:4 states, *"Greater is he that is in me than he that is in the world."* We did not understand all that God was doing but we knew that there was a great change in our lives and Christ made the difference. God had to work on both of us. He needed to get me to a place where I would totally depend on him regardless of the circumstances. I needed to be able to look past the situations and see God so while I was home, I spent my time in His word reading and praying. On the other hand, my wife was very independent. She needed to get to the place where she would accept me as the head of the household. It would no longer be her calling the shots and making all of the decisions. God designed man to be the head of the house and that is the way it had to be. One afternoon, my wife called me from work stating that she had been hurt on the job. The injury would cause her to be out of work for several weeks. While she was in the process of explaining what happened a call came in on the other line. I asked her to hold on while I answered it. An employer was on the other line offering me a full-time job. God works in mysterious ways!!

With my wife working we had only one vehicle. My father had a pick-up truck that was just sitting in the yard not being used. My brother wanted to buy it from him, but my mother said "No, because Boot, (which is my nickname) will need something to drive when he comes back to church." My mother had faith to believe that one day I would return home, so my father complied with her wishes. It is good to have a praying mother who puts her trust in God. Hebrews 11:1 says, *"Now faith is the substance of things hoped for and the evidence of things not seen."* The Lord began to bless me and as a result, my father gave me the truck at no charge. God will change the hearts of people even when they are not saved (like my father). He saw my life change from who I was to who

God would have me to be. The Lord gave my father a compassionate heart to help anyone in need.

There will come a time when God test your loyalty to one another, the ministry, and to Him. He wants to know where you stand moving forward therefore, testing times will come. This was bigger than God just bringing us back together. It was about working for the kingdom so that souls can be saved. Our motives must be pure, and we must remain humble and willing in the process. I went to my pastor one day and we discussed marriage. He informed me about what to do. I responded I am doing all that I can" and his words were, "Do more." Sometimes we look for the easy way out like the children of Egypt. I did not move too fast or too slow in the process but moved as God moved us forward. As we grow in relationships with God His inward voice directs our steps. I worked on me, she worked on herself, and God worked in the middle. From this point on in our life, we will continue to confront challenges that lead us to our divine purpose. Zechariah 4:6 states, *"Not by might nor by my power, but by my spirit saith the Lord of hosts."* I tried my way for a long time, but it got me nowhere and my downs were greater than my ups. I realized that I had to be the first partaker of the process because God has given the authority to man to step out in faith and leave the rest to Him.

I never was one to take orders from others, but I had to humble myself to the almighty God if I wanted things to change. There were times when I had to cry because didn't know what to do but wait, depend on, and trust God for everything. I got tired of being a failure. Humbling myself allowed me to focus on being the best in areas that would benefit the ministry and believe me, it was not easy. The temptation to stray into other people's lanes or areas would sometimes cause problems. It's just like starting life all over again and growing up the second time. Jesus said to Nicodemus in St. John 3:3, *"Verily, verily I say unto thee, except a man be born again he cannot see the kingdom of God."* People fail to realize that once you backslide you must do your first work over. God wants us to get it right so we can reflect His glory and goodness and show His love to everyone around us. We are all unique in the body of Christ; different members but functioning as one unit. Your light will illuminate everyone around you.

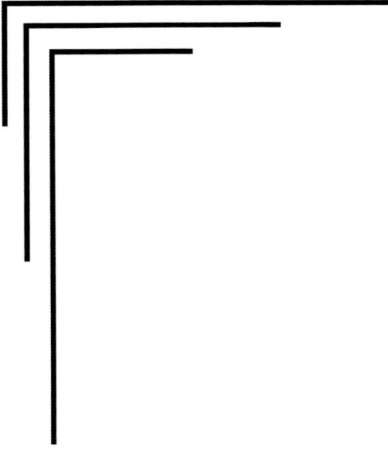

"Therefore if any man be in Christ, he is a new creature: old things are passed away; behold, all things are become new."

2nd Corinthians 5:17

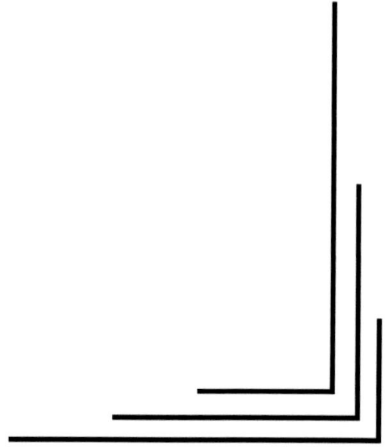

Chapter Three

Timing is Critical

Our pastor used to say that you cannot hang around everybody but try to find people that are striving to move forward in their spiritual growth. Their words carry weight and can set you up for success or failure. Mentors are a precious gift from God. However, there are times when we just need to talk to God because He understands everything that we go through. Because of the lifestyle I chose, I found myself back at my parent's home. This was very hard for me considering the fact that I was once on my own and my only source of transportation was a bicycle. It was also a humbling experience, and no one trusted me even though my life had been changed. Everyone was on pins and needles. All they remembered was the old man. They couldn't seem to accept the new creature that I had become. 2nd Corinthians 5:17 says, *"Therefore if any man be in Christ, he is a new creature: old things are passed away; behold, all things are become new."* Regaining trust and confidence takes a long time to reestablish so, I had to be patient. As I waited, it seemed like things would get easier!! I was wrong, things actually got harder but that is the cost of saying "Yes."

When I said yes to God it meant that I was turning my life totally over to Him. 2nd Corinthians 1:20 states, *"For all the promises of God in him are yea, and in him Amen."* Little did I know the challenges ahead or the opposition I would face while moving forward. God had me in a place where I had no choice but to trust his decisions. Proverbs 3:5 states, *"Trust in the Lord with all thine heart: and lean not unto thine own understanding."*

During the time that God restored me, we were in the process of building a new church. My wife and I were also in the process of rebuilding our relationship. I believe that God wanted to work on our relationship before we entered the new sanctuary. I got involved in working in the church, going to Sunday school, and Bible study. These were things that would help to develop and mature me spiritually. I had a love and passion for Sunday school and became very involved. At times, there were things I didn't understand but I never gave up. As time went on, I became a member of the "Praise and Worship" team. I realized that there is a price to be paid for leaving the safety of the church and start to do fleshly things. I had low self-esteem, lacked control, and I worried about how people felt about me. There truly is a war going on between the Spirit and the flesh, but I had to fight. I thank God because 2nd Corinthians 2:12 states, …. *"When I am weak, then I am strong."* *God had really changed me, and I knew it!!*

Staying focused means not paying attention to distractions because they get you off course. Anything that happens that is not part of your goal is just a distraction. Often the full plan of what God has for your life has not yet been revealed. So, in my preparation time, I had to remain patient and trust that God knows what He is doing.

As a result of my previous lifestyle, I spent 30 days in a rehabilitation center. I met people from different places and different backgrounds. I was in a place where I felt all alone and hopeless. I worked in the program, and it gave me hope but not deliverance because I didn't realize that God was in the midst. After being released when I thought that I had everything under control, "Look out!!" I stopped working on the program, relapsed, and went back to using again, however, this time I cried out to God and He delivered me from the drugs and alcohol that had me bound. He freed me!! God has given me a fresh start and I am so glad He did.

People watched me for a long time to see if I was really serious and although the devil tried to tempt me on different occasions God gave me the strength to overcome. There were times, if I may be truthful that I failed God, but I picked myself up and got back in the race again. I was not favored in my home, family, or church but there was one person I could count on at all times and that man was Jesus Christ. The quality of your life is based on the quality of the choices that you make. I had to learn to accept what God allows.

This will start a new chapter in our lives and a new move of God as He leads us. Doors that seemed to be shut God opened. The people had a mind to work, and souls were being saved by the power of the Holy Spirit. I encourage you to remain aware of God's timing, not your own or anyone else's when stepping up and taking on more responsibility. The Bible says in Proverbs 18:16, *"A man's gift makes room for him and bringeth him before great men."* There will come a time when your pastor or a spiritual leader will say it's time for you to move forward into the plan of God.

My agenda and focus were to please God with all my heart. Feeling blessed that God uses your testimony and your life to be a blessing to others is a humbling experience. I started out on the praise and worship team, and I gave my all to the glory and honor of God. There were times when the Holy Spirit would come into the church and people's lives were transformed by the power of God. Others may try to urge you to rush ahead and get in front of God, but you must remain humble.

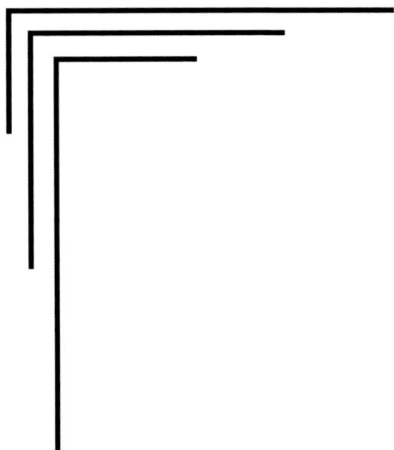

"But Jesus beheld them, and said unto them, With men this is impossible; but with God all things are possible."

Matthew 19:26

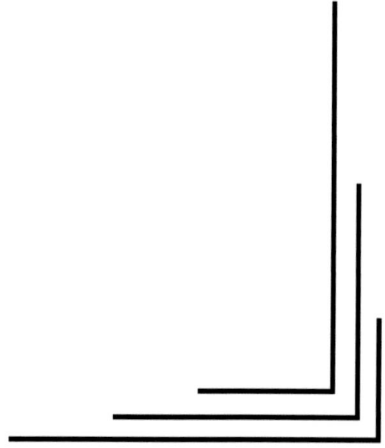

Chapter Four

Marriage Under Fire

It has often been said that "experience is the best teacher" and I am a firm believer that this is true however, there are exceptions to every rule. As my journey began, being raised in the church and knowing church protocol and the order in which things should be done, I learned life skills and how to incorporate scripture into my daily life and grow in grace. This will work if you hold on to what you have been taught and trust in God for His direction. As we know, once you start to get older things change, especially the way you think and feel about how things should be done. When you drift away from the path of righteousness you are heading for a life of destruction. When I departed from the church things started working out just as I expected. They say that the grass looks greener on the other side but "Beware" because you are in for a rude awakening. In the beginning, you have many possessions, money in your pocket, so-called friends, and the pleasures of life. You meet someone, fall in love, and things are good for a while.

As a backslider, I started getting involved in things that the devil had to offer simply because they were appealing to the eyes and the flesh. My life became chaotic and out of control but as a result of God's infinite grace, mercy, and His unconditional love, He gave me another chance. My brothers and sisters began praying for a turnaround in my life and God answered their prayers. God blessed my wife and I to move into an apartment together with only one income. We were poor naturally but spiritually rich in God. We were on our way. We attended church every time the doors were open, praying together and listening to the teaching and counseling of our Bishop. With no job and my wife working God made ways for us that would be impossible for man to believe. Our pastor counseled us about trusting God, working together as a team, and giving God all the glory and we did just what he said.

We rode this roller coaster for years; up and down but little by little things started to improve. The love of God's Word gave us a feeling of hope and restoration. Our pastor instructed us that we can be victorious in Christ Jesus and one day be able to help someone else that was just like us. We listened attentively to him as he spoke. The Bible speaks about how Mary pondered it in her heart. We pondered it in our minds. So, we suffered, not being able to have some of the things we desired such as: a new suit, shirt, dress for my wife or even being able to get her hair done without postdating a check but we survived. Even though it is painful to suffer, it is good because it brought us closer together. We also began to focus on what we did have versus what we didn't. Many times, we only had enough money to pay our tithes, put an offering in church, and put gas in the vehicle to go to work. It was hard but we had one another and God; that was the joy of it all. At this time, we were both working bringing home a paycheck and little by little things started to change for the good. Nevertheless, our credit was bad. We depended on God for everything that we needed whether large or small. Little is much in the Master's hand.

We were trying to purchase a better vehicle, so we went from lot to lot with no satisfaction. My wife desired to have a Mazda 626 and one Sunday after church as we passed the dealership and there it was right up front, and it was as white as a cloud in the sky. So, with no money and bad credit, we went to inquire about the vehicle. The salesman was very nice, and it seems that God sent him there just for us. Long story short, with no money and bad credit God made it possible for us to get the car that we wanted, and we picked it up the next day. Matthew 19:26 states, *"With God all things are possible."*

My job was not full-time until after 90 days of service and there were only two shifts: day shift and second shift. They said if I wanted to be full-time the only shift available was the second shift. I declined and let them know that the second shift would interfere with my church services. Because I believed God and wouldn't take the first thing that was offered, God opened up a third shift just for me so that I could attend my church services. If you hold out and do not give in, God will open up doors that seem to be shut. People laughed at me and thought I was crazy, but I believed in the power of God and what He will do if you trust Him.

God didn't just stop there. As time passed God blessed us to be able to build a new home. It was truly miraculous because our credit was terrible however, God touched the hearts of the financial institution just as if they had blinders on their eyes. We experienced a move of the Holy Spirit in ways that would literally blow the minds of the unbelievers. Jesus told Peter to "come" and he walked on the water. Just come believing that God can and will do according to His Word. Little did I know that God had a plan for us as it reads in Jeremiah 29:11, *"For I know the thoughts that I think towards you saith the Lord, thoughts of peace and not of evil to give you an expected end."*

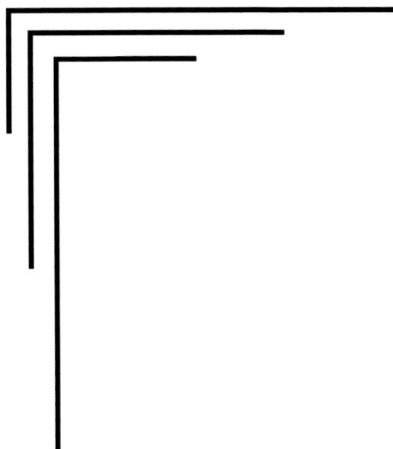

"Trust in the Lord with all thine heart; and lean not unto thine own understanding. In all thy ways acknowledge him and he shall direct thy path."

Proverbs 3:5-6

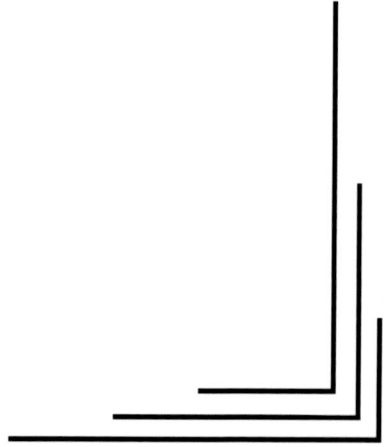

Chapter Five

Marriage and Family/

The Husband-and-Wife Relationship

Growing up in a home with six siblings I often watched how my parents interacted with one another. I didn't understand fully the marital relationship between a man and a woman, but I did know a little about love and respect. There was always something special about having a father and mother and the family being together. As I grew older, my mother joined the church, however, my father did not. For a brief period of time, things seemed to be working fine because marriage is about working and doing things together. Little by little things started to change. Arguments would automatically surface for no reason at all, if it wasn't this it was that; two people with different agendas. Therefore, my father did his thing and my mother carried us to church. Church brings about a separation between right and wrong, so they were unequally yoked. At times, the children were caught right in the middle of the chaos. Nevertheless, I still believed that there was something special about being married. Every now and then my father would attend church but never committed himself to joining in his earlier years. It was during his latter years as his health started to decline and he was unable to come to church that he accepted Jesus Christ into his life before God called him home. After the passing of my father, I would stop by Bishop Cooper's house and as usual, we would just talk but on this occasion, he said, "Can I call you son" and I said "Yes." There was such a feeling of comfort that I just couldn't explain. The love behind those words was so powerful that it brought tears to my eyes.

We continued to attend church regularly and through the Word of God, our family learned God's purpose for our lives. As we grew older, we had the right to choose to follow one or the other (my mother or father). The church was fun and exciting. We learned about who God was, sang in the choir, and played different instruments. What a joy it was knowing who Jesus was and that He gave His life for us thousands of years ago. The Bible is a life-changing experience and will help you in difficult times in your life. During our high school years, we encountered students from different backgrounds and different lifestyles which can potentially have a tendency to sway you in the wrong direction. They make it seem as though you are missing out on having fun just because you go to church. Feeling as though I had to prove myself, I got involved with the wrong things and the wrong people. Peer pressure causes you to be between a rock and a hard place. This happens to nice people frequently when they try to "fit in." When your desire is to be a part of the "in crowd" your standards are lowered. So, who I was and whom I became had a split personality; one side knew to do good, and the other side knew to do bad. I chose to enjoy the pleasures of life for a season; just like the prodigal son did, not realizing that God was with me all the time. When I changed partners, my life began to spiral downward. It is just like giving a child a new toy. He is overjoyed for a while.

The good times lasted for years but that feeling of husband and wife and marriage never left me, so I got married and it was great. No marriage is perfect, there will be problems, and disagreements will come. You must be able to come together and work through the problems or they will continue to grow. Working together coupled with communication is the first step in building a successful relationship together which includes much give and take.

God put man and woman in the garden to be fruitful and to work together as a team to accomplish His will, but sin interrupted God's plan for man. You cannot do this on your own. You need the help and the power of God to succeed in life. Marriage is the foundation of who Christ really is according to the Bible. All of the teaching and preaching that I have heard over the years as I was growing up helped me to see that without God I will fail. This was the lesson that I learned later in my marriage. We are going to go through things, but God will give you peace, joy, and love to work it out together. Once Christ became the center of the marriage things began to slowly work out. It was hard but with God, all things are possible if you believe that He can do it. Once you leave the ark of safety the devil begins his attack on your life. The Lord has been a blessing to us in so many ways and has blessed us to be a blessing to others along the way. We still have our moments from time to time, but God is in control now. Jesus can do what may seem hard and impossible for man but there is nothing that God cannot do if you believe and don't doubt. Our marriage is now built on a rock and that rock is Jesus Christ. We are now working on God's plan, and it is great to know that He is in charge of our lives. We still have a long way to go because the journey is not without sacrifices. I am eternally grateful that God did not let me die in my sins. He allowed that dream of marriage to become a reality. God placed man and woman to be the focal point of life and happiness. God told Jeremiah, "I know you." It is great that God knows you and His way is the best way.

The Lord has allowed my wife and me to be in a place where we are able to help married couples who feel like all hope is gone. There is hope in Christ. God has blessed us with a testimony of His power, grace, and forgiveness. There was a time when our marriage had gotten to the place where my wife and I were constantly arguing and complaining. It seemed as though we could never come to an agreement on anything. At this point, she was just fed up and wanted out. She had become angry and bitter. One day at work, a couple of the friends that I associated with told me that they saw my wife going to the lawyer's office. I was shocked because I had no idea that she was even considering divorce. She had all of the paperwork drawn up and attempted to have them served to me, but the address was incorrect, so I never received them. We are an example that divorce is not the plan of God, but man. God is a God of second and third chances. Every day that our eyes are opened our life with Christ is renewed and we are given another opportunity to be witnesses of who He is and the wonderful things He can do if we are willing and obedient to His word.

There was a co-worker, a brother in the Lord that I talked to on a regular basis. At that time, I was going through some difficult times in my marriage and so was he. Bishop Cooper was instructing me concerning my marriage according to the truth of God's Word. As I gained strength from listening and being obedient God allowed me to help my brother. He and his wife were dealing with communication, and finances, and were just not getting along. We would talk about the Lord every day at work, but this day was different. He wanted to know how I felt about divorce. According to the Bible, divorce is not in God's plan. It is easy to get up and throw in the towel, but we must be fighters to the end. Love doesn't give up it causes us to fight for what is right. I understood what he was going through because at that time I was experiencing the same things. He listened but he chose to leave. He was gone for about two weeks and returned home to his wife and has been living happily ever after since that time. He has two children that have graduated from college, his wife has her Doctorate Degree, he is retired, and the Lord has called him into the ministry.

There was a time when the Lord blessed us to get credit cards. Instead of using them to benefit us, we abused them. What could have turned out to be a "good thing" ended up being a learning experience of what not to do. We suffered for several years trying to erase our debts and God blessed us. We said we would never end up in that predicament again but, guess what!! We did it again. This time, however, we learned some very valuable lessons that came with much suffering. Proverbs 3:5-6 states, *"Trust in the Lord with all thine heart; and lean not unto thine own understanding. In all thy ways acknowledge him and he shall direct thy path."* We failed because we did not consult God. At this point we became good stewards with what God had provided for us and as a result we were then able to help someone else. We encountered a couple that were struggling with their finances. We were able to share our story with them so that they would not make the same mistakes. Life lessons can be difficult, but they are designed to benefit others.

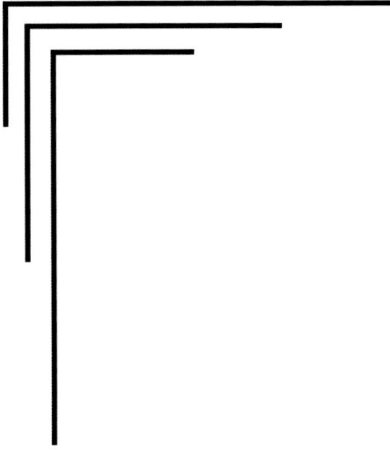

"Come now, and let us reason together," Says the LORD," Though your sins are like scarlet, They shall be as white as snow; Though they are red like crimson, They shall be like wool."

Isaiah 1:18

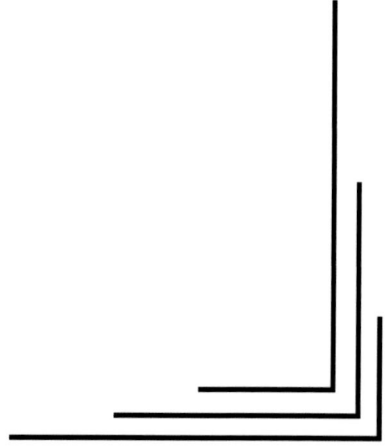

Chapter Six

The Struggle is Real

Wanda Floyd

Growing up, my parents had a very loving relationship. My mother was an educator, and my father was in the military (Army). He later became an educator as well. They were both educational and career driven. I had one sister that was four years older than me. In my junior year of high school, I got pregnant and had a son. We lived at home until I graduated the following year. I went to college, so my parents continued to care for my son while I was away. They were truly a blessing to me. I grew up in an era where children were taught about values and morals and premarital sex was definitely not an option. There are consequences when we decide to do what we choose and go against the teachings that have been instilled in us through our parents. I was at the age where I felt as though I could do what I wanted but that always comes with a price. College only lasted for two years. My father got very ill, I came home and never went back. He died shortly thereafter. My son and I moved into an apartment. We didn't have an abundance of material possessions, but we had a lot of love. I began working two jobs to make ends meet.

My now husband of 37 years and I lived together two years prior to marriage. In the beginning, things were good even though we were from two different backgrounds. He was a backslider (once saved), and I was a churchgoer (never saved). He was a member of a Pentecostal church, and I attended a Methodist church. I was a single parent with one son who was ten years old at the time. I was very independent and accustomed to doing my own thing. I was in control (so I thought) and felt as though I didn't have to answer him. For years, I had been making my own decisions. I was in a bad place and didn't realize it!! We eventually got married so, the two became one, and the child became ours. Although he did not have any biological children, he accepted my son and raised him as his own; but I still had my opinions. At this point, things should be getting even better but they actually got worse. We separated for a while but when we reunited, I was saved (the Lord was working on me) and he had rededicated his life to Christ. I had to learn to let God lead and let my husband be the head of the household. God began to chip away at that stony heart and turn it into a heart of flesh and little by little we developed a healthy marriage. Our marriage is not perfect. We are two different people and disagreements will come. Isaiah 1:18 states, *"Come and let us reason together…"* As a result of being obedient to the Word of God, He restored peace, joy, and oneness.

For many years I have developed a passion for helping people and as time goes on the desire has continued to grow. Kindness is giving hope to those that think they are all alone in the world. I have come to realize that my gift is the "gift of helps." The Lord has blessed me with a kind and compassionate demeanor and the ability to encourage people. Kindness is not what you do but it is who you are. Who wouldn't serve a God like this?

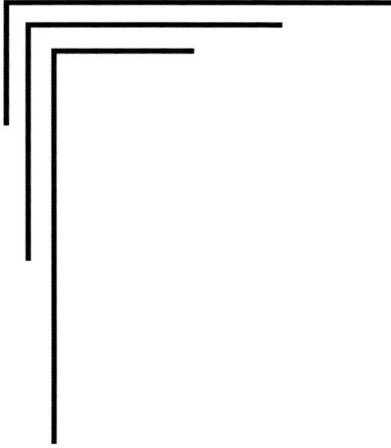

"Knowing this, that the trying of your faith worketh patience."

James 1:3

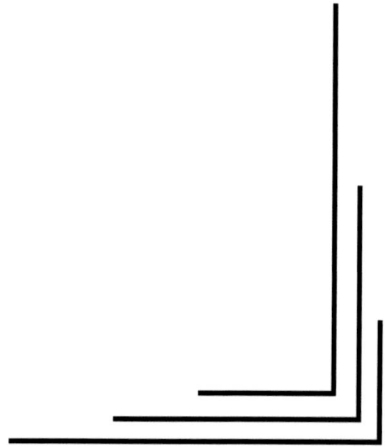

Chapter Seven

Meditation, Prayer, Fasting and Study

For years I struggled with the idea of trying to live a disciplined lifestyle spiritually and naturally. I would start but not finish. Life itself brings about many issues that put a great demand on my family and social life. However, before pointing the finger at others, I had to look at myself and determine what is causing me to become distracted when it comes to living a disciplined lifestyle. I faced so many distractions on a daily basis such as e-mails, texts, and Facebook just to name a few. Most important is the explosion of information technologies of this day but deep down inside I longed for peace, love, and happiness. The world has not changed; the people have. In Ecclesiastes 1:9, *Solomon says, "there is no new thing under the sun."* If you are to be disciplined, first you must identify the problems that hinder you. Take a moment, slow down and breathe, and ask yourself the question, "Who am I in this crazy culture?" The Bible says in Jeremiah 6:16, *"Stand ye in the ways, and see, and ask for the old paths, where is the good way and walk therein."* Discipline builds in your inner peace, joy, and freedom that only God can give. When God transforms you, a change comes that produces the fruit of the spirit.

Discipline is not something that happens overnight but is a slow process that may take days, weeks, or even years. James 1:3 says, *"Knowing this, that the trying of your faith worketh patience."* We must read, study, and meditate upon God's scriptures. Jesus was disciplined in memorizing His word and expects us to do the same. As we understand God's Word, we will have victory over the devil. When Jesus was led into the wilderness to be tempted by the devil, he won the fight using the power of the scriptures. A life of discipline is not just for pastors, priests, or prophets. It is for ordinary people like you and me. The list is great, but the reward is greater with God. A disciplined life brings power to your ministry and carries out the plan of God. We cannot operate on knowledge alone we need the power of the Holy Spirit. Prayer establishes our relationship with God as He leads and guides us in all truth. A spiritual life that is disciplined helps us to move away from the shore and launch out into the deep. In St. Matthew 4:19, *Jesus said, "Follow me and I will make you fishers of men."*

The generation of today is so much different from the generations of old. The older generations just did what they were told to do (not questioning at all). However, today's generation needs an answer and precise instructions on how and why to do everything. Spiritual discipline starts from the inward part of the soul and changes the attitude of the heart. We must remember that it is not the path that changes us, it only places us where the change can occur. Whatever we do must be done to the glory of God and not man.

Prayer and fasting brings us into a relationship with God's plan for our lives. Prayer and fasting along with meditating on the word will make a change not only in you but in everyone you meet. Prayer places a yearning in our hearts to desire to know more about God and his word.

Studying helps us to understand God's plan for us so that we lean not to our own understanding. We must acknowledge him in all things. If we genuinely love people, it will cause us to pray that God's will be done in their lives. We are covered by the blood of Jesus and sealed because he gave his life for our sins on the cross. Biblical fasting always focused on spiritual things. The normal way of fasting involves abstaining from all food, solid or liquid. In most cases, fasting is private between the person and God. Fasting must be centered on God and initiated by the Holy Spirit and God ordained. Simplicity gives us the freedom to praise and worship God in the spirit of holiness. The only way to get to believe and have faith is in the book. It tells us that you shall know the truth and the truth shall make you free. Comprehension is the next step up in the discipline of study. Concentration centers the mind and keeps it focused on your studies. When we repeatedly read, study, and meditate we will start to think like Christ.

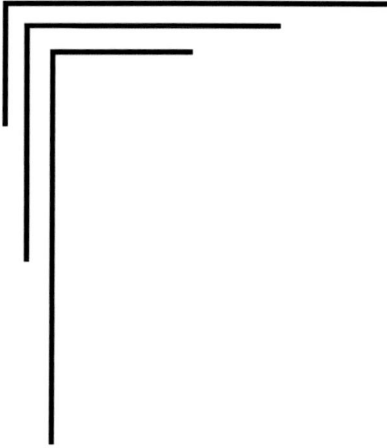

"And ye shall know the truth, and the truth shall make you free."

St. John 8:32

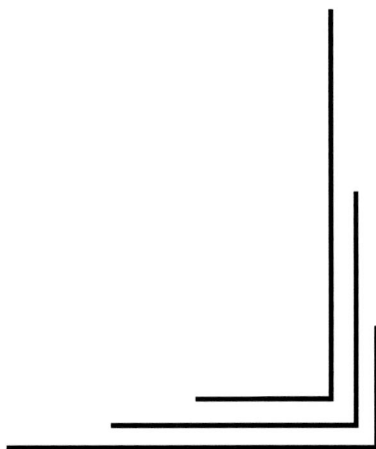

Chapter Eight

"What is Truth?"

Many people in today's time are skeptical because of the atmosphere of distrust and because people are altogether giving up on the truth. I believe that truth is the reality that is presented to you as facts that are real in its nature. I asked myself, "Can we get by without the truth?" The world we live in has so much dishonesty, hatred, and violence that people are losing their identity. The true meaning of truth can only be found in the Word of God. St. John 8:32 states, *"And ye shall know the truth and the truth shall make you free."*

One thing I can say about the truth is that it has a voice and can speak for itself. I experienced the truth at my job. A few years had gone by, and everything was going great until one day the Human Resources representative called me down to the office. Sometimes things in your past will come back to discourage you from moving forward in the Lord. The H.R. person and I sat down and discussed the unpaid taxes that were outstanding from my past, informing me that they would have to garnish my paycheck. I asked how much they were going to take, and she said, "half of your weekly salary." My response was, "the Lord will provide." She then said, "how are you going to make it?" and I replied, "I will be alright." I sensed the concern on her face but there came a peace on the inside that let me know it was going to work out for my good; just keep trusting in the Lord. I stopped by my wife's job to let her know what happened and she said, "it is going to be alright." After I got home, I received a call from H.R. letting me know that everything had worked out. God is good, He worked things out to where I never missed one paycheck in 25 years until I retired. Favor isn't fair but when you trust God and stand on the truth you are on the winning team.

I had worked six years on the third shift when a day shift position was posted along with a promotion. There were three other co-workers and I that applied for the position.

After the interview process was over there were two applicants considered: me and another co-worker. As we waited for the outcome, the co-worker informed me that if I was chosen, he was going to quit. This was nothing but a distraction to make me feel defeated but what God has for me is for me. Not only that, but I also had truth on board. I was chosen. God blessed me with the position and guess what!!! The co-worker did quit.

We must realize and understand that God is who He says He is based on the Bible. A few years ago, there was a movie called, "A Few Good Men" starring Tom Cruise and Jack Nicholson. Jack Nicholson told Tom Cruise, "You can't handle the truth." The truth is that maybe we can't. Truth disputes the fact that someone is right, and someone is wrong. Everyone has their conception of what truth is, nevertheless, the Bible is right, and somebody is wrong. People just want to go with the flow, not really concerned one way or another about the truth. I thank God for this five-letter word (truth) that means God's unmerited grace. God's truth says that His love is unconditional regardless of how we treat Him. Truth is not an idea, game, or puzzle. It is a person living in you instructing you how to live.

When people argue about things that they believe are true they become dogmatic, not recognizing the fact that this is only their opinion; not necessarily the truth and set themselves up for failure.

The truth helps us to treat one another right and respect their opinions. If an act is wrong for one, it is equally wrong for another.

Proverbs 22:6 states, *"Train up a child in the way he should go and when he is old, he will not depart from it."* The training that I received on truth growing up never left me, when I strayed from God His truth was still with me. So, when things got really crazy, I had something to lean on and that was the truth. It's one of those mind-stretching truths to consider that God, as the Creator created time and yet is not subject to it. There was a time when my son and grandchildren came to stay with us briefly. He was not saved but attended church with my wife and me. He started asking questions about God's truth so we would stay up into the wee hours of the morning talking because he became hungry for the Word of God. During those times I learned to remain flexible and to look for what the Lord may be trying to teach us. First of all, I knew he wanted a change, and that God didn't just send him here to visit but to help him experience a life of freedom through his parents. Sometimes the unexpected arrival of a calamity leaves us dazed and disoriented with times when we feel paralyzed and don't know how we will even move forward; then God sends us help!! My son is a nice young man that lost his direction just like I did. You see, it's often your response in those moments of crisis that determines how you will make the most of your time. Being led by God is essential. I never truly was a father, so I had to learn and ask God to help me be there for him and share the things that I have learned. How you respond is how you are going to be received and that's why the truth is so important. I am convinced that ultimately patience requires faith. We would all sing, study the Sunday school lessons, and pray together. God was turning things around in his life and his children's lives. God was bringing us closer together as a family. This was just what I needed. If we had chosen to have regrets this would prevent God from blessing and using us for His glory, so we had to stop and reset our hearts to the truth. Each day became a fresh start with a willing heart to serve.

Portrait of my Dad

My father is a strong, kind, loving and
Passionate man
Always willing to take on any situation at hand
When I am weak or fall, he lifts me up so that I
can stand
A good father like him, it's hard to find that
brand
He always strives to satisfy and please
"the Lord"
A soldier at arms who carries his bible like a
Sword
He's in sync with his wife like music to a chord
And always keeps his family on one
accord
There's a lot of things that I want to say
Like, Lord shine your light and have your way
To have a father such as you, I have
Always prayed
You are a blessing, so just shine because
"This is your day!"

Author: Dennis B. Watson

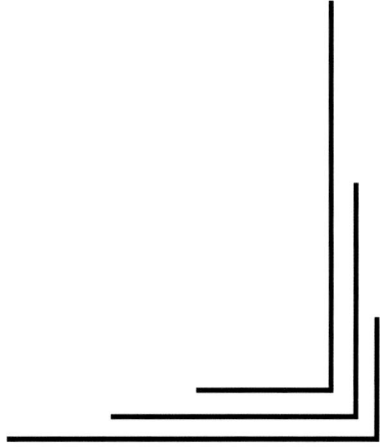

Chapter Nine

Relationship

In the beginning, God made man in His image and established a relationship with Him. His plan was that man and woman would come together and produce offspring but because of sin, God sent His son to redeem man back to Him. I strayed away from God and severed the relationship between my family and the direction that God had for me. I thank God for His redemptive power that saved me from sin and death. It's amazing how we can think that life has no consequences so, we take things for granted and lose every-thing. My concentration now is on God first, my wife, and the church family that He has blessed to be a part of my life. I am grateful for my relationships because they connect me with people that I know and some that I don't but, in the process helps me to develop and mature.

I realized that love is not just sexual or two people coming together but true love is a bond between husband and wife. Love is one of the most profound emotions of human beings. Romantic relation-ships comprise one of the most meaningful aspects of life. Love and relationships are forever. That's just my thoughts on the matter. My relationship failed because I did not put in the time and effort that it took. I put my friends and family before my wife. To be suc-cessful it is often necessary to go outside of one's comfort zone such as: buying flowers, making a date, or even buying chocolate candy, and doing whatever it takes to get the ball rolling. For me, it was hard, but I didn't give up. I was willing to do whatever it took. With the help of God, our relationship took a leap of faith as we depended on Him. Relationships need the freedom to speak and follow your heart in order to please one another. We are two differ-ent people but that's a good thing because we were able to come together and reason. Isaiah 1:18 states, *"Come now, and let us rea-son together..."* Even being married there are times that you desire to be single because of immaturity and not considering the full responsibility and weight that marriage carries. For marriage to truly work it must be founded upon the Word of God. Our attitude often makes the difference between success and failure. God wants the marital relationship to be a total success. Why is that? It's because He wrote the book!! Through years of experience, God has shown my wife and me how to go from defeat to victory one step at a time. The enemy's job was to discourage us, but God encouraged us through His Word. Television shows such as: Leave it to Beaver and the Cosby Show paint a pretty picture of relationships and how they live happily ever after; but they are just entertainment!! I had to understand that neither of us are perfect, and we never will be in this life. We must receive understanding and patience from God and finish this race with joy. We ofttimes use the word charity which means love. Love is giving and not taking. In some relationships people spend more time complaining than helping and when we are actually honest with ourselves, we find that we complain all of the time. As I looked back over my life, I realized that I complained about things that didn't even make sense. Instead of being part of the solution, I became part of the problem.

What is said and how it is said determines whether or not your mate is convinced that you are sincerely trying to help them with their weaknesses. There was a time my wife and I went to seek counseling from our Bishop concerning our marriage. As we were sitting there talking, he was listening, and I went on a rampage talking about how she should act according to what the Bible says in reference to her behavior. I said nothing about myself or my attitude regarding the situation. So, Bishop took out his notepad and wrote one word. It was "approach." Instead of helping the situation, I was making it worse. That one word made me feel like I had lost my best friend and from that time on, my life was changed. What I failed to realize was that if I hurt the one that I loved that I was destroying a part of myself. For a real breakthrough to come into your relationship, you must learn to forgive and forget past failures and mistakes. No marriage or relationship will ever succeed until both parties forgive as Christ forgave. Our weapon for winning was love. Galatians 5:22 states, *"But the fruit of the spirit is love, joy, peace, longsuffering, etc."* There was a time when our relationship was built on feelings but now our marriage is built on the Word of God.

There is nothing that can take the place of praying in faith on a daily basis for the one you love. We must have balance in our homes, on our jobs, and in the church. This is vitally important to a healthy home and marriage. There is a certain fellowship I can share with my wife that she cannot get from anyone else. This was ordained by God for it was He that joined man and wife together.

We all need to be built up not brought down. If you begin to speak words of encouragement and commendation through patience, you will begin to see the Holy Spirit at work in your relationship. Philippians 4:13 states, *"I can do all things through Christ which strengthened me."*

I experienced a communication separation in our relationship due to the fact that I nitpicked all the time and as a result she just shut down. Communication plays a key role in a healthy relationship. It's important to talk about more than just parenting and maintaining a household. We needed to strive to get to know one another in a deeper sense. I lost connection because I became disconnected from her needs and from her as a person. Keeping concerns and problems to yourself can breed resentment, lack of confidence, and low self-esteem. What I had to learn was that women respond to how they are being treated. Find a middle ground and build from there. To disagree does not say that you are wrong or right. Marriage is about understanding and moving on. Sometimes you just have to agree to disagree. Disagreements are a part of all relationships. This is how you grow together. Our relationship was lacking physical, emotional, and intellectual intimacy. All couples need intimacy in different forms to grow closer and those are the things people want to hide under the rug. We had gotten to the point that we could not talk or even listen to one another so we were just in the house together saying nothing to each other and I know that there are marriages that can relate to that!! I am thankful because I can see how it was then and how it is now with the help of God.

I can remember when we first got married; how nice and polite we were to one another. After years had passed, we started taking one another for granted and disrespecting each other. It is so easy to do. I have heard people say, "I love my spouse, but I am not in love with them." How can we as believers think this way when God is love? You can win with God on your side. I thank the Lord for my marriage and relationship. God showed me that just because you see marriages fail doesn't mean that it has to happen to you, but you must trust Him through the process. I did just that and look at us now. We went into the fire, but we don't smell like smoke. Our smell today is victory!

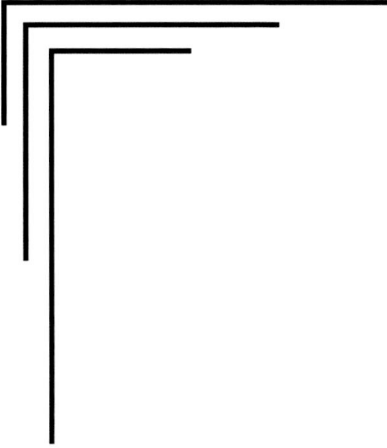

"For the king knoweth of these things, before whom I speak freely: for I am persuaded that none of these things are hidden from him; for this thing was not done in a corner."

Acts 26:26

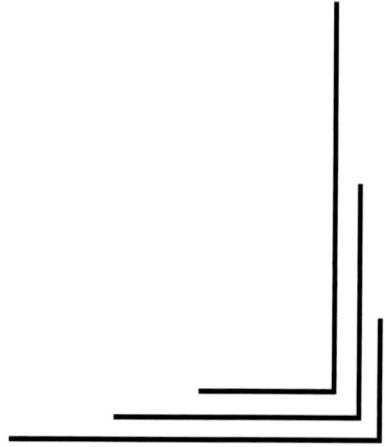

Chapter Ten

Embracing Your Mission

What does the word mission mean? According to Webster's Dictionary, a mission is the sending out of persons by a religious organization to preach, teach, and convert. It is the life and mission of the church to emphasize the baptism in the Holy Spirit as God's provision empowering the church (believers) to proclaim the Gospel and also Jesus' ministry. God's word was not meant for just one area or just one person but for the entire world to know who Jesus is and the purpose of His coming. As Paul was speaking to King Agrippa in Acts 26:26 he said, *"For this thing was not done in a corner…"* meaning that it was done for the whole world to see. We as believers have a duty and responsibility to fulfill God's plan for every man, woman, and child and to spread the gospel through the power of the Holy Spirit. In times past things were different because resources were limited however, today they are unlimited making them available to everyone who believes in Christ and is called to work in the vineyard.

We are to shake entire cities, countries, and nations through the power of the Gospel. Godly men and women prayed fervently for the people and mighty signs and wonders followed them. Demons were cast out, healing took place, and the sick were made whole again. God has given us the authority and boldness to proclaim liberty to a dying world. The apostles and the prophets of old started the work of a missionary and we are to continue until the day Christ returns for His church. The duty of kingdom work extends further than the four walls of our local church. I am an ambassador for the kingdom and the importance of witnessing our mission is critical because we are running out of time. Jesus is on his way back for his church. There are thousands of souls that are still lost and have not heard the gospel. St. Matthew 28:19 tells us to go, and to teach all nations baptizing them in the name of the Father, and of the Son, and of the Holy Ghost. The primary responsibility of missionaries is to go out into the hedges and highways and compel them to come.

What does the Gospel do? It enables me to take a closer look at my life and examine myself. The preaching of the gospel centers around repentance and remission of sin (in other words forgiveness) and becoming separated from the old lifestyle and being renewed by the Spirit of God. This will make men disciples of Christ and obedient to his commandments. The purpose is not just to enlarge the membership but is designed to make disciples that are willing to separate themselves from worldly lifestyles and be transformed heart, mind, and soul. We must understand that there is a life after this, heaven or hell. We must open our eyes to the truth about heaven. 2nd Peter 3:9 states, "It's not my will that any should perish, but that all should come to repentance." Our mission is to love, care, and help the lost be found through God's word. We must embrace the "whatever it takes" attitude so that we will be victorious. The Bible says that he who wins a soul is wise. You must be willing to give of yourself totally to the work of God. The apostles and the prophets were talked about, lied on, and even robbed. Some of them lost their lives for the sake of the gospel nevertheless, they did not stop moving forward because a person that is motivated by the Spirit cannot be stopped. If we would all join together and towards the same goals soul will be saved and delivered from the bondage of sin. St. Mark 9:23 states, "All things are possible if you only believe." Let us briefly look at the apostle Paul's life. He was a persecutor of the church. He knew the law, but he didn't know Jesus. One day he met Jesus on the road to Damascus, his life was changed forever, and he became one of the greatest missionaries in the world. We must become motivated and dedicated to the mission set before us, not afraid of the dangers we may encounter as we visit other cities, countries, or wherever God sends us. Jesus called us out of the darkness and gave us the assignment to proclaim the gospel to all of the world. He made it personal because that is what he does; one on one.

In the beginning, God made man and he was special. He formed him from the dust of the earth, breathed life into what was still, and made him alive. The awesome power of God should cause every church to support and stand behind the missionary outreach. Jesus gave his life so that man could be victorious through his death. The fire that we need to minister to the people comes from the Holy Spirit. On the Day of Pentecost, the Spirit filled the place and everyone there began to speak in other tongues and as a result of that great move, three thousand souls were saved. We must help unbelievers to receive this by faith in God's word. Anticipate that God is going to move and open up doors for the mission but most importantly, have a plan and stick to it. The gospel is the message of Jesus Christ and must be made clear and plain so that it can be heard and understood. You must realize that being a good or a nice person will not give you salvation. You must be born again through the blood of Jesus (just as I was).

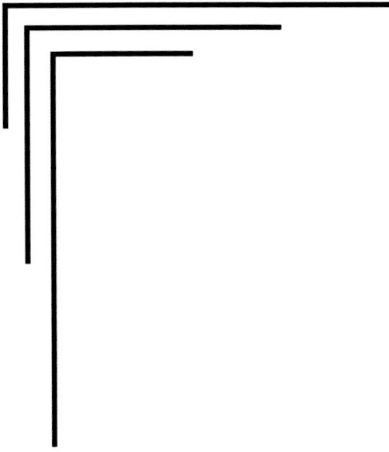

"And the Lord said unto the servant, Go out into the highways and hedges, and compel them to come in, that my house may be filled."

St. Luke 14:23

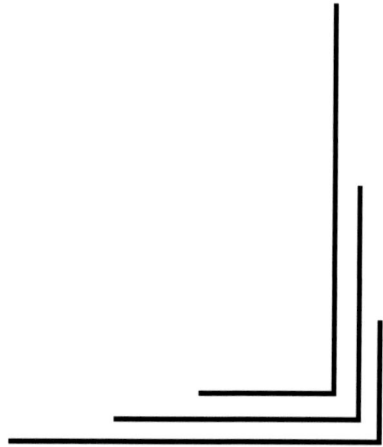

Chapter Eleven

Changed Without Regrets

I realized that there is a real war going on between the spiritual and the natural life that we live. I thank the Lord for the change that took place in my life. Now I can see clearly and understand through God's Word His plan for our lives (me and my wife). St. Luke 14:23 states, *"And the Lord said unto the servant, Go, out into the hedges and highways and compel them to come in that my house may be filled."* There are people that need to hear the unadulterated word without compromising so that souls can be saved, set free, and delivered by the power of the Holy Spirit. I believe by not truly understanding the Word of God that the devil took advantage of the situation and slowly but surely, I drifted away from God and the people that loved me. Most of all, I thank God for giving me one more chance to get it right before he comes back. My prayer was, Lord teach me how to live according to your Word and to love my wife just as the Bible says. Everything you do or say comes with a price. You must be careful what you ask for because testing times will come. I thank the Lord for being patient with me. As days turned to months and months to years my relationship grew stronger and stronger. Did I suffer? Yes, but it was all for the good. I am truly on the battlefield for my Lord.

 The things that came my way challenged my faith and increased my confidence that no matter what I faced God was in the middle with me. Today, I am not led by the natural man but by the spiritual man. 1st Corinthians 2:14 says, *"But the natural man receiveth, not the things of the spirit of God for they are foolishness unto him, neither can he know them because they are spiritually discerned."* Situations and troubles are designed so that we gain faith and build trust enabling us to realize that He will see us through. What a friend we have in Jesus. He loves us even when we fall and is right there to pick us up and move us forward. He will never leave you alone. I have learned that He is always there. Even during the times when we think He is not, He does things to let us know that He is.

Just writing this passage, I can feel His spirit as my words are being expressed on paper. When you think of His goodness and venture down memory lane and reminisce about how far you have come you must be mindful that without His grace and mercy, it would not have been possible. It has been over thirty years since the Lord restored me and I have no regrets. Every morning I wake up to his new mercies and joy that fills my soul. I have a new life with a fresh start because this is the day that the Lord has made, and I shall rejoice and be glad in it. I am so grateful that my ending is not like my beginning.

Every morning before I went to work, my wife and I prayed for God's protection as we went through the day. When I entered the parking lot at my job, I prayed that my light would shine before men and that they would see Christ living within me. I loved my job. I was a welder for twenty-three years and I carried the characteristics of Christ each day but that's not to say that I was perfect. I had people tell me I would never amount to anything, and I started to believe them "But God!!" He let me know that it wasn't what people say about you, it was what He says about me that matters.

Since I chose to believe God versus what people said, my wife and I are still married, and we are both retired. The Lord took a person that was down and out and raised him up and He didn't stop there. God blessed me to receive my Doctorate degree. Just trust Him through the process and watch Him work.

I believe God placed me on that job to bring about a change; first in my life and then in other people's lives. As I look back over my life, the things that I experienced, the suffering I endured, and even the ridicule I received were to make me a better person. God was making me and molding me into what He would have me to be.

The Lord allowed me to become a station leader in a welding department on my job. That was an experience that not only taught me how to work one on one with the welders but also to become a team player with the group of men. I learned how to listen, to be humble, to be there when I was needed, and to learn that everybody is different. We were a team, working together and achieving much. There were times when we had to work overtime, and I worked right along with my team to get the job done. God didn't stop there. He allowed me to build and invent fixtures to help the job produce more work using fewer people to save time and increase production. As a result, I was awarded a silver star award from the company plus a bonus check for a job well done. They are still using those fixtures in the company today so you can't tell me what God can't do if you walk upright before Him. God will raise you up to be the head and not the tail. Looking back, God had me on the potter's wheel and little by little He was taking out the imperfections. I didn't understand the process, but I trusted God and the work He was doing in my life. Commitment means that there are no strings attached.

I talked about God's forgiveness of sins and His free gift of grace to anyone that was willing to listen. The Bible tells us that the only way we can love others is because we know the true source of all love which is God. When you stop and think about the fact that God loves you it doesn't make sense; not logically or rationally. Isaiah 55:8 states, "For my thoughts are not your thoughts, neither are my ways your ways, saith the Lord." I realized that God didn't need me, I needed Him. Who would have regrets knowing a God that gave His life for people that didn't deserve it but deserved death? God demonstrated His love just for me and yes, I must be selfish because it is personal.

It's this freedom and this power that fuels me to lead and serve selflessly. For about two years I was thinking about retiring; planning and getting excited as the days approached. I know how I carried myself around the job. I started thinking about the way I thought people felt about me so, I just wanted to go to work one day and announce that this is going to be my last day!! I told my wife what I had decided to do, and she said that was not a good idea. She went on to say that God has been good to you. All of the years that you have worked there and all of the lives you have touched, do the right thing and leave with integrity. On the day of my retirement, the job gave me a party. My wife and my cousin came to support me. The office staff, welding department, supervisors, and station leaders all came to celebrate my last day of work with me, and it was a great day for me. I thank God for having a wise wife that loves me so much. I was not trying to win the approval of man. My goal was to be pleasing to God. The gift will cost you, but the rewards are priceless.

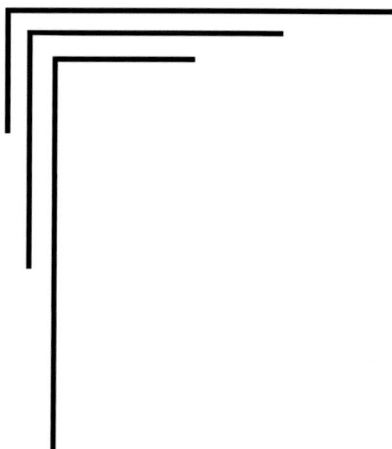

"Husbands, love your wives, just as Christ loved the church and gave himself up for her."

Ephesians 5:25

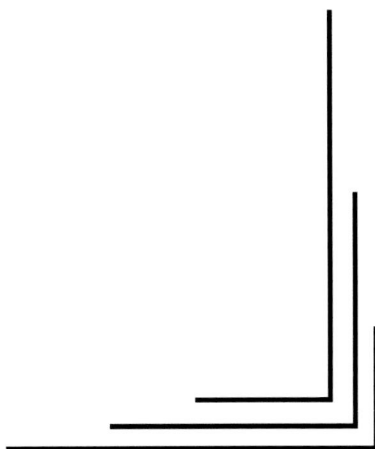

Chapter Twelve

Marriage Vows

Marriage vows are the promises that two people make to each other during a wedding ceremony before God and other people as witnesses. It is declaring a lifetime commitment to one another. The clergy asks you both to face one another and repeat these words. I (the groom) take you (the bride) to be my wife, to have and to hold from this day forward, for richer or poorer, in sickness and in health, to love and to cherish for all the days of my life.

God takes the covenant and vows very seriously whether you are a believer or not. Making vows in God's name when you do not really mean it is a serious thing. When my wife and I started to date, I had left the church. In other words, I was a backslider. Before we got married, we lived together for a while. She had a son when I met her. We all got along great and had good times, so we decided to get married to complete the union. I always thought marriage was special and it was something I looked forward to. The thrill and excitement of marriage if not taken seriously can be destructive. After a few years, things started to happen, and little things turned into big problems. Instead of getting closer, we started to drift apart. I did not just let myself down but also my wife and son who looked up to me for support, strength, and protection that I seldom showed. I was thinking about myself, my feelings, and how I was being treated and that does not work in a marriage. This is what I saw growing up, living at home between my parents; how selfish they were to one another so, when I got married, that same mindset became a part of me.

Fast-forwarding the story, when the Lord restored me back into fellowship, I asked Him to teach me to love my wife and teach me His ways. Ephesians 5:25 states, *"Husbands love your wives even as Christ also loved the church and gave himself for it."* It was just like starting all over again but this time I wanted to get it right. I knew it would be a fight, but I was "in it to win." I believe marriage brings joy but also challenges that can be worked out with the help of God. First, we had to listen to someone that had some wisdom and life experience. Hebrews 13:4 states, *"Marriage is honorable…"*

Bishop Cooper often said that women respond to how they are being treated and that is a fact. There are so many marriages that are failing, and we did not want to be a statistic. I believe that God uses our experiences to help people in need. For example, God has placed in my heart a passion for marriages to be successful. Too many people are just throwing in the towel and giving up on the most beautiful life that God has provided. I thank God for the change that took place before it was too late. The devil works hard trying to destroy the works of God, especially the relationship between husband and wife because when two come together nothing can stop them. We are both retired and can see how God is bringing us closer and closer together. Each day we wake up with new mercies, joy, peace, and a new love for one another. *Proverbs 18:22 states, "Whoso findeth a wife findeth a good thing, and obtaineth favour of the Lord."*

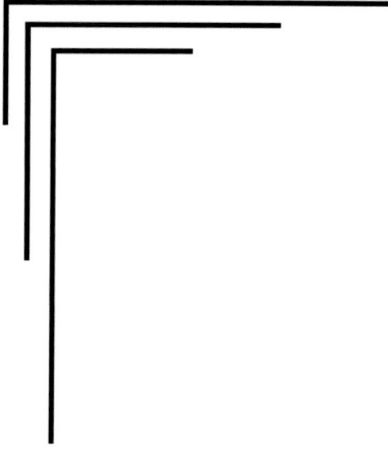

"In all thy ways acknowledge him, and he shall direct thy paths."

Proverbs 3:6

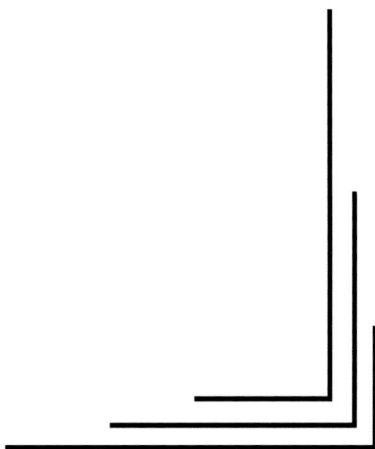

Chapter Thirteen

Fresh Start with a New Beginning

After years of faithfully serving God with your whole heart, you ask yourself the question, "What do I do now?" The best thing to do is to stand still and wait on God. As His Word says in Proverbs 3:6, *"Lean not to your own understanding, in all your ways acknowledge him and he shall direct your path."* Basically, you are giving God permission to participate in every decision and move that you make; not being guided by what you think. God wants to give you the best, so that is why it is important for us to pray and receive His plan for every situation in our lives.

I had the desire to attend bible college, but I wasn't sure if that was a part of God's plan for my life. I talked to Bishop Cooper and explained to him how going to school would enable me to help the church and he said, "That would be a good idea." When God has placed a desire in your heart to do work for him, here comes the devil placing doubt causing you to feel as though you are not qualified for the task. You must believe what the bible says about fear in 2nd Timothy 1:7, "For God has not given us the spirit of fear, but of power, love, and a sound mind."

When you are serving under a leader that wants the best for his people you want to strive to follow in his footsteps. He has received his degree. Psalm 37:23 states, *"The steps of a good man are ordered by the Lord and he delighteth in his way."* When you give of yourself faithfully, you may not receive the reward but generations to come can look forward to it because of your service. There are so many people looking for things that will benefit them but not benefit the Kingdom of God. Acts 20:35 says, *"It is more blessed to give than to receive."* My goal is to give back to God with loving service. The Lord has allowed me to give my best without trying to compare and compete with others, trusting that what He has for me is greater than anything that this world can offer. I found a college nearby and attended once a week. The instructors and the students were friendly and willing to help me reach my goal. I didn't even know how to write a paper, but I trusted God through the entire process. Obstacles, conflicts, and problems that seemed too big for me were not too big for my God. When negative thoughts came into my mind telling me to quit, God said to keep moving. He knows what is best for us. My attitude and my thinking had to change; I was in college. I thank the Lord for my chancellor who recognized that I was teachable, willing, and able to learn through obedience and hard work. I told my wife that if I just got a "C" I would be satisfied and she said, "That is not acceptable." I wanted to do just enough to get by and she knew that so, I thank the Lord for my wife as she encouraged me along the way.

There are so many people in the bible that came from obscurity and didn't necessarily see themselves as worthy of the roles in which God placed them. Abraham and his wife Sarah struggled to believe God, Moses tried to refuse God at the burning bush, David, the shepherd boy was anointed by God and so many others. God is not looking for the most talented, most educated, or even best looking but the one that will trust and depend on Him. So, when my attitude slipped, or I began to succumb to feelings based on circumstances, I had to walk by faith. Faith requires us to look beyond what we can see and how we feel. Hebrews 11:1 says, *"Now faith is the substance of things hoped for and the evidence of things not seen."*

As the work got harder, I started to feel frustrated, powerless, and even cried at times but that small still voice on the inside said, "Trust me." The challenge was maintaining the right attitude in situations that felt so wrong. Love keeps trying, remains patient, shares everything, and never gives up. While we cannot control our emotions, we can limit the impact and influence they have on our attitude. Right thinking will always lead you out of tight squeezes and into the light of God's truth so, I had to work through my seasons of pain. During the process I learned that perseverance will always outlast persecution. The bible states in Jeremiah 1:5, *"Before I formed thee in the belly, I knew thee."* God already had a purpose and plan for our lives, and it is our responsibility to embrace it without questions or reservations. By doing this, we will see that what is impossible for man is possible for God; if we trust and believe Him. So, I had to become a man of integrity, someone willing to do the right thing and obey God no matter what, or who was looking at my life. My first year of bible school was the hardest but God allowed me to pass, and I was grateful. Little did I know that Bible study and Sunday school were preparing me for bible college.

I am so glad that I had an old school Pastor that believed in the "old time" way. Many churches are moving away from Sunday school (teaching) and how it develops your life for ministry and spiritual growth in God's Word. Before I truly understood how valuable Sunday school is, I was having a conversation with an older Pastor and was sharing my spiritual desires. All I wanted to do was to help someone along this journey so that my living would not be in vain. The words that I spoke set me up for a life-changing experience. What I didn't know then, I know now. I was speaking life into my future. Today, our need for the Bible, and God's Word is more important than ever. Our world is bombarded with ideas, however well-intentioned, that challenge the time-honored concepts of the God of the bible.

In order to help someone, you must study God's Word. 2nd Timothy 2:15 says, *"Study to show thyself approved unto God, a workman that needeth not to be ashamed rightly dividing the word of truth."* That way, when people come to us with a question, we are able to give them an answer. There were times when I started studying God's Word at night and it would be two or three o'clock in the morning. I was scheduled to be at work by 7:00 a.m. but God strengthened me. He knew that was what I needed. As I look back over the things I encountered, now I can see God in every step of my life.

While I was completing the second year of my Associate's degree, I was also working on the first year of my Bachelor's degree and teaching Sunday school. They said it couldn't be done but I serve a God that can do the impossible. The scripture becomes meaningful to you when your heart is open and illuminated by the Holy Spirit to guide you in all things. Jesus asked Peter the climactic question, "Whom do you say I am?" Peter's response was, "You are the Christ, the Son of the living God." The Bible does not become the Word of God, it is already the Word of God.

When I worked on my job, I would always challenge myself to do better, and the same principle works in the spiritual. Step out in faith and believe in God. We have a choice. We can open our minds and heart to the Holy Spirit and allow the Word to become personal in our lives. This was a test of faith and trust in God. Did I get frustrated? Yes, I did feel like giving up and throwing in the towel but the spirit on the inside would say, "you can make it." Our faith is rooted in the Bible, but we don't worship it; we trust it. When you explore God through His special revelation you build your own personal foundation and information bank. Our personal concept of God, when we pray, for instance, is worthless unless it is coherent and coincides with His self-revelation. As you grow in

Christ you learn that you are not making the decisions; it is God, He knows you. Nothing surprises Him for He knows your very thoughts. Everything that happened to me that was good, God did it. There are times you may feel that God does not understand or know what you are dealing with but Jeremiah 29:11 says, *"I know the thoughts that I think towards you...to give you an expected end."*

There are times when you will get off track, but it does not surprise God. Consider the man who walks east into a strong east wind and turns around and walks west. The wind was on my face, but now it is on my back. There has actually been no change in the wind. It was his direction that changed. You must keep your focus as you walk in the middle with God. You have to realize who you are and who God made you to be and remain true to your identity. God blessed me to graduate with my Associate's degree in theology and work toward my bachelor's degree. To God be the glory for the plan that He has for me. Isaiah 40:31, *"But they that wait upon the Lord shall renew their strength. They shall mount up with wings of an eagle, they shall run and not be weary, and they shall walk and not faint."* God wants you to soar and he will use the wind to blow you wherever you need to go. Don't look behind you or below you. Look up and ahead and stay focused on God's guidance.

There are times the devil tries to say you are disqualified because of your past or what people say or think about you and if you believe it, you will actually disqualify yourself. Remember, you are a work in progress. There was a time when I wasn't true to my word, now when I say something I must do it. Your word is your bond and is as important as your name because it identifies who you are. My mission is to love serving others as Christ did. It's a joy knowing that you can change a person's day from being gloomy to being happy. Serving is the key to success. Your thoughts forecast the future. *"For as he thinketh in his heart, so is he…"* Proverbs 23:7 You have to walk by what you know about Christ and not by what you see. In your lifetime you will always go through transitions and seasons. In my season of change, God has allowed me to receive my bachelor's degree, but He didn't stop there. I also retired from my job at the age of sixty-one years old. Only God can do the impossible. I thought that this was the end of my studies but encouragement from my chancellor and my wife motivated me to finish what God had started. I pondered it in my mind and pushed forward to pursue my Master's degree with God leading the way. This was my season. I was preaching, teaching Sunday school, writing papers for class assignments, and completing projects. I realized that higher heights meant harder trials to face. My purpose had not yet caught up with my passion.

Going to bible college caused me to think more outside of the box concerning God's plan for the kingdom mission instead of just church work inside of the building. When you seem to be different it's because you have changed and in so doing have come into a different relationship with God. St. Luke 12:48 states, *"For unto whomsoever much is given, of him shall much be required..."* Because God is a person, you must stay in communication with Him at all times. Although God is a spirit, without a physical body, He is nonetheless real. In all my life studying to receive my Master's degree was unbelievable coming from my past lifestyle and the things I was involved with. God sees our past and future. We cannot change our past, but God can make our future glorious for His purpose.

On the day of my graduation to receive my Master's degree my wife, my mother, and I were sitting in the car waiting to enter the church. My mother opened her purse and handed me a little black case that had my father's diamond ring in it. What a surprise that was!! I was speechless. She said, "I was waiting to give this to you at the right time and this is the time and the place." Galatians 4:4 says, *"But when the fullness of time was come, God sent forth his son..."* Two weeks before graduation I did not have my grade point average or test scores, so I was concerned. My wife said, "Don't worry, it is going to be all right." The big day is here!!!

Graduation day has finally arrived. We all gathered together to march in, and the chancellor walked around handing out medallions to different graduates and they said Summa Cum Laude. I had no idea what that meant. The lady standing next to me said, "That's the highest achievement you can receive in college." I just responded and said, "Okay." I didn't know that I was at the top of my class. I was amazed!! God hid that from me to keep me humble. Ephesians 3:20 says, *"Now unto him, that is able to do exceeding and abundantly above all that we ask or think according to the power that worketh in us."* I did my best and God did the rest. Deep down inside I had no clue as to what God was doing. All He said was to trust Him and He would finish the work that He started, and He did.

After all of the struggles and hardships that I have been through, I did not graduate from high school but a few years later received my diploma, God took a nobody and made him somebody for His kingdom. People used to ask me during my early days if I was a minister, but I just served as a maintenance man around the church and was happy. Colossians 3:23 states, *"And whatsoever ye do, do it heartily unto the Lord, and not unto men."* I loved working in the yard planting flowers and shrubs making the outside of God's house beautiful. I discovered the satisfaction that comes from serving others even when you don't realize it at the time. We must remember the strength that God has given us is not just for us personally; it's so we can be strong in someone else's life.

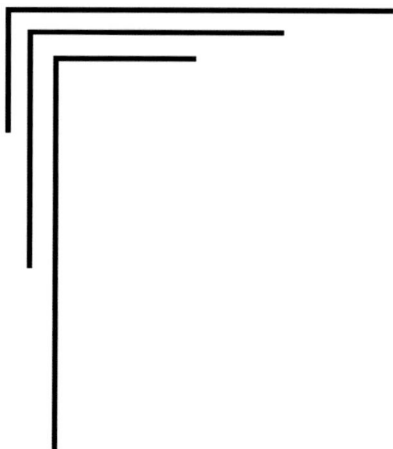

"And this is the confidence that we have in him, that, if we ask any thing according to his will, he heareth us:

And if we know that he hears us, whatsoever we ask, we know that we have petitions that we desired of him."

1 John 5:14-1

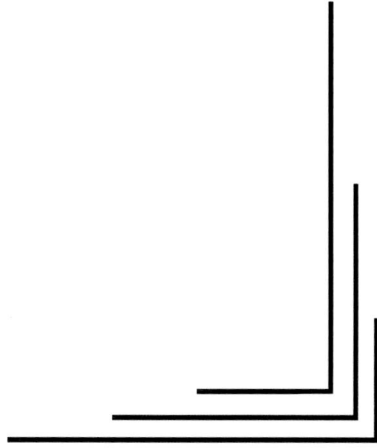

Chapter Fourteen

My First Steps

There is nothing that will bring you such confidence as a life that is well pleasing to God, but it cannot be achieved until there is a perfect union between you, God, and Jesus. 1st John 5:14-15 states, *"Now this is the confidence that we have in Him, that if we ask anything according to His will, He hears us..."* The moment you pray, the heavens are open so, what makes you lose confidence is disobedience to God and His laws. Romans 10:17 states, *"So then faith cometh by hearing and hearing by the word of God."* There are times when there seems to be a stone wall in front of us, but you cannot give up. You must have the devotion and conviction to believe that he will not and cannot fail. Being born into the new kingdom is being born into a new faith. Being saved is one thing but totally trusting God is another and this was my very first step in believing that Jesus died for me. The things that I experienced built my faith and confidence because you cannot talk about things that you have never experienced.

God has a process of training you for what your future will embark on. First, God must have control of your life. There are things that need to be broken and bad habits that need to be changed. Most importantly, we must be sure to take time and communicate with Him every day. When I first began thinking about bible college, I wanted to be sure that it was God speaking and not just a feeling. When there is love in your heart there is no room to boast about yourself. God gets the best out of you when you become like little children because he can shape and mold you to glorify him. 1st Peter 1:7 states, *"That the trial of your faith being much more precious than gold that perisheth..."* I read a book years ago by Smith Wigglesworth, a man that could not read however, he was a powerful man when it came to faith and God used him mightily. I had to learn to take my eyes off of the conditions and symptoms no matter how bad they may be and get them fastened on Him. You often hear people say, "I am waiting on God but if the truth be told, God is waiting on you. When a man is born of God he is brought from the darkness into the light. That is a magnificent miracle that only God can perform. Miracles are occurring every time we open our eyes in the morning; they are called "new mercies." There was a time that I was coming home from work and on my way, I fell asleep at the wheel. When I opened my eyes, I was heading right into the back of a car so, as I veered over into the other lane somehow, I ended up facing traffic. There was no accident. God blocked it!! What a mighty God we serve!! The devil's job is to steal, kill, and destroy God's people. Miracles are still happening. Philippians 2:5 says, *"Let this mind be in you, which was also in Christ Jesus."*

During the time I started working on my Doctorate degree, I was challenged, tested, and it seemed like the suffering increased. At times I felt alone and wanted to give up. The devil will play with your mind. That is when you cry out to God for help that only He can give. Little by little, God through His Word and prayer brought me through. If you open the door to God and access your faith God will move on your behalf. St. John 14:12 states, *"If ye shall ask anything in my name, I will do it."* You will have whatever you ask for if you believe it in your heart, speak it, and don't doubt it.

Proverbs 18:21 states, *"Death and life are in the power of the tongue and they that love it shall eat the fruit thereof."*

There are times when it seems that God is silent and that's what I didn't understand. In these times He wants you to use what you have been taught and trust His Word for His Word is true. You must remember how gracious God has been in the past and the wonderful things He has done for us all. If we can just keep these things at the forefront of our minds our faith will be strong. You cannot be in close contact with Jesus and receive His Word by faith and not be affected in your body, spirit, and soul. I have seen God heal people from cancer, diabetes, and broken hearts and spirits; those that were unemployed and bound by circumstances were all freed by the power of God. We must learn to gain faith through past experiences. Jesus wants us to stand on the "solid rock" and that rock is Him!! Men are searching everywhere today for things to replace God. The answer that they are looking for is right in front of them with arms wide open. I found Christ in the "book," and He is the one I need for my spirit, soul, and body. For you not to believe God, what has He done for you not to?

It is important that every day you lay some new foundations that can never be uprooted. You shall arise with a new impartation of power and a deeper sense of His love (so are you excited yet?) I have been retired for about three years and have not been bored one day but wake up to enjoy Jesus. I realize that suffering is just a part of who we are and it's a good thing. God is trying to get us to leave the shoreline. There is only one place where we can obtain the mind of God and that is when we launch out into the deep. I believe there is a close relationship between you and Jesus that no one else knows about. Jesus said in St. John 14:27, *"Peace I leave with you, my peace I give unto you: not as the world giveth, give I unto you."* God has blessed us all with gifts and talents to be used for His purpose. They were there before you were born but when salvation comes into our lives God expects us to use them for the kingdom of God. No matter what your gift is, the more you exercise it the better God can and will use you for His glory. Then one day you will hear the Lord say, "Well done thou good and faithful servant, you have been faithful." This is what I want to hear the Lord say to me.

God will always bless you as you store up heavenly riches for the advancement of the kingdom. Our culture puts so much emphasis on status symbols such as luxury and success, but these do not reflect success in the eyes of the Lord. Success is making the most of what God has blessed us with. In order for God to give increase to our lives, those fleshly desires and self- promotions must decrease. I know from a personal standpoint that a closed door simply means something inside of me must be developed before I can enter the throne room of God's grace. One of the major ways to unlock your gifts is through serving. Draw close to someone who is already exercising similar gifts. Birds of a feather do actually flock together. Not everybody is able to help you during your process. Make sure you are connected to the right people.

Jesus ascended to heaven to prepare a place for us. He clearly told the disciples, *"In my Father's house are many mansions: if it were not so, I would have told you. I go to prepare a place for you. And if I go prepare a place for you, I will come again, and receive you unto myself."* (St. John 14:2-3) All Christians should look forward with deep anticipation to the return of the Lord for them and what a great day that will be. As that day approaches you must continue making yourself ready to meet Him. It is true, the cross of Christ is paramount to human history. When we grasp the full meaning of what Christ's death has for us, we can join all creation and declare that He is worthy to receive or worship. I worship because I am grateful that Jesus released me from being a slave to sin. He paid the price that freed me through His blood. The truth of Jesus Christ dying as our substitute is so prominent throughout the bible and so awe-inspiring that it cannot help but bring you to heartfelt reverence and thanksgiving. In our final analysis, the Lord knows those who are His and the cross is God's gift to all who have received

Him. God demonstrates His own love for us. Romans 5:8 states, *"While we were still sinners, Christ died for us."*

 The first step to salvation is believing God's plan for you and allowing God to do a deep cutting away of the unbelief. His ways are perfect. Jesus will always send you to the right places. My desire was to give back and help those that had fallen and felt there was no hope. My wife and I got up one morning and decided to visit the rehabilitation that I once attended. What an exciting moment in my life to give back to help someone in need. The gospel is not about you, it is designed to be given away. The lost are those that do not believe. To all who believe, God's plan is clear, I will when you will. Therefore, my mission is to go into the hedges and highways and compel men and women to salvation. We started on our journey to Warwick, Maryland. This is something that I have desired to do for a long time. There is a special feeling that comes about when doing something for God. When He places it in your heart the day is brighter and the joy of working together is amazing. What more can you ask for? We arrived at our destination, got out of the vehicle, and began to just look around at the place where I once was. The water shined beautifully over the lake but this time I was not a resident; I was a visitor. All the glory goes to God who freed me. We went into the Administration office to explain the purpose of our visit. I had been a resident there some years ago and

I wanted to give back by sharing my story of success with the hope of encouraging someone that was just like I was at one time. The director of the rehab said that because of COVID-19 many changes had taken place and people, and their families are not allowed inside the building at this particular time. There was still a ray of hope; he said that this situation would gradually change over time. This may seem to have been a failed trip but not so. I did what was in my heart and when one door is closed another one opens up. We left, had lunch, and enjoyed being together. It was the right thing to do, and God was with us.

The Holy Spirit will make us witnesses for Christ, ever proclaiming that Jesus is our Lord and our Redeemer. There was a time when my wife and I could not travel long distances together without arguing but now we are able to go anywhere peacefully sharing the good news of Jesus Christ. Assurance of salvation should not lead us to indifference and smug contentment. It should lead us to deep joy and a loving response to Christ as we continue to trust Him. You must remember that you are not your own but are bought with a price. The gospel is not Christ and something else; it is Christ alone. You are distinct and unique from the rest of creation. Take a look at yourself; there is no one in the world exactly like you. Genesis 2:7 states, *"The Lord formed man from the dust of the ground and breathed into his nostrils the breath of life, and man became a living soul.*" That is why you matter so much to God. You are a part of him. The sin of Adam and Eve, as we have seen, was something for which they were personally responsible. They did not have sinful natures such as we have so the temptation of sin must have come from an outside source. Genesis 3:1 declares that the serpent who was very subtle was used by the devil to alienate them from God by using deceptive words. There are times when we may think, "Why didn't God stop and prevent Satan from bringing evil into the world since He knew in advance what would happen? God's plan was for man to live in a relationship of love with Him, however, man could not love if he was not free. God gave man a choice (free will). He did not want man to be pro-grammed like a robot, He wanted mankind to serve Him with a pure heart. There is no love like the love in the spirit. It is a pure, holy, and divine love that is poured out into our hearts by the Spirit. The Word of life is the breath of heaven and the life-giving power by which you are changed.

Some years ago, my wife and I went on vacation to Charleston, South Carolina where she grew up. While we were there, we attended an old-fashioned camp meeting. As the people were praising and glorifying God an older missionary approached us. She had never seen us before, but she said," God is going to bless y'all. May I pray for you?" We said yes, but little did she know that we were looking for a house. After we returned home, we ventured out looking for a home. God had placed a desire in our spirits to pursue our dream with no money and bad credit so, we moved forward. When you are motivated by the Lord, nothing can stop you. Just as Peter walked on the water, he asked Jesus," If it be thou, bid me come unto thee on the water." It was not about the money or the credit, it was about faith and believing that God can do it because He has all of the resources that we need. God sent a realtor our way named Shirley. There was only one lot left and it was in the development we desired to live in. We believed that it was ours and by faith, we sealed the deal that day. This was in 1996 and we are still living in the same residence as of 2023. Good is so good!! Hebrews 11:1 says, *"Now faith is the substance of things hoped for and the evidence of things not seen."* When you trust God and don't doubt, He will turn your dreams into a reality.

There is a place of confidence, assurance, and rest where God has perfect control over all human weaknesses. You are able to say that I know all things are working together for my good. The spirit of the Lord has shown me that God is looking for people who can see that from the foundation of the world He has had them in mind. God has delivered us from many difficulties that have come our way and is strengthening and equipping us with divine boldness through His almighty power. Romans 8:31 states, "What shall we then say to these things? If God be for us, who can be against us?" Yes, the struggle is real but are you going to let the past which God Himself has worked out for you bring you to a place of distress? Or are you standing during your testing times quoting God's Word? God will set people right before you to show His miraculous power and we will not believe, so what is it going to take? Jesus is on His way back for His church so let us prepare for His arrival!

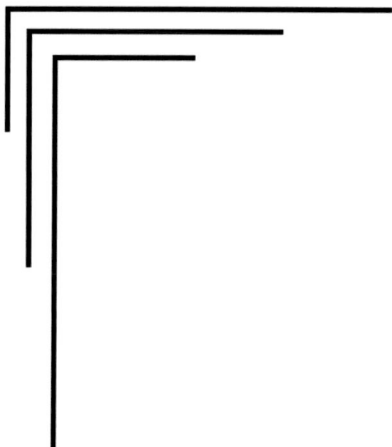

"Surely I was sinful at birth, sinful from the time my mother conceived me."

Psalm 51:5

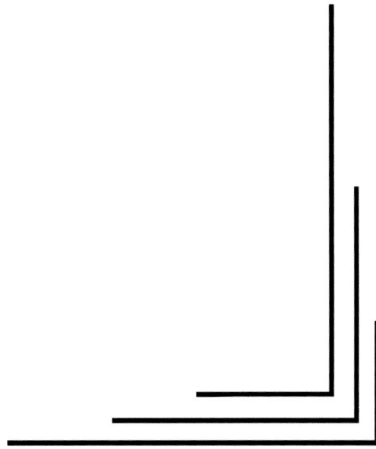

Chapter Fifteen

Best Time of My Life

God has always wanted the best for His children but because of sin, man failed God yielding to the voice of Satan. God sees the beginning and the end and turns things around for His good. We are always on the winning team with Christ. Psalm 51:5, states *"Behold, I was shapen in iniquity and in sin did my mother conceive me."* What makes you special to God is when you surrender your life to

Him. Job 23:10 states, *"But He knoweth the way that I take; when He hath tried me, I shall come forth as gold."*

I did not start off badly. I grew up knowing right from wrong, respected my parents, and during my earlier years did not get into much trouble. By the time I entered high school things started to change. I met people that had cars and worked part-time jobs. It seemed like they were having a lot of fun and living the "good life." This was all new to me because on Friday nights I was in church, and they were either at a basketball or football game or just riding around with a friend that had a car. As soon as I got a car, things really did change for me. I could go, and I had a part-time job. I believe my life turned around when I got out of high school and started working on my first full-time job. I had money to spend!! All people are not equally bad, and God knows this very well. Romans 3:23 states, *"For all have sinned and come short of the glory of God."* We use this to do things that we want to do but in relation to the holy, sovereign God, we all come short. There are times we begin to reason in our minds (between the ages of 18 and 21) and it seems like a light has come on. It becomes easy for us to shun a discussion dealing with sin and treat it rather lightly referring to them as big sins and little sins. Sin is more than just self-centeredness. Only God's view can give us a true perspective. He is the one who designed us and gave us the rule book. When you start getting involved with people who have no rules you are headed for a dead end. The fight occurs when you know the difference between right and wrong because there comes a time when you must choose. We have done those things we ought not to have done and have left undone those things we ought to have done. Sin regardless of the type will always bring about disastrous consequences. You actually think no one will know and that you can get away with it. You must always remember that there is a God that sits high and looks low and He knows everything that goes on. The story of the prodigal son found in St. Luke 15:11, states how he left home, journeyed into a far country, and wasted everything he had, having a good time. This is my life!! I spent all of my money, had no place to go, and no one gave me anything. So, one day I was sitting in a place of loneliness, a place where God could get my attention. At that moment, I got up and asked God to help me because I could not help myself. I came to Jesus just as I was, hurt, broken, and damaged. This was my time and season for a miracle. Jesus was right there, and He rescued me. There is one thing that I know. When it seems as though you are all alone, He is right there. He didn't leave me, I left Him. Because His love reaches down in muddy places, He found me. The Bible teaches us that we have eternal significance in God's eyes and that our souls are worth more than the whole world. St. Mark 8:36 states, *"For what shall it profit a man if he shall gain the whole world, and lose his own soul?"* As I began studying the Bible, I found in Jeremiah 3:14, *"Turn, O backsliding children, saith the Lord; for I am married unto you..."* It is amazing how God shows us in His Word just how much He loves us. God, Himself has provided a plan and a purpose that He has for each one of us. The choice is our responsibility as individuals to respond to Him. His will is for us to live in His presence forever rather than in everlasting separation from Him. This is why I can say that this is the "Best Time" and season of my life being in Christ because it could have been totally different. I could have been in prison, dead, handicapped, divorced, and my mind could have been messed up. God blocked all of those things from happening to me. God has allowed my latter days to be better than my beginning. I thank God for my suffering. It has made me stronger and wiser, and I trust Him in all things. When I learned to trust Him fully and say, "Not my will, but Thy will be done" the frustration was removed. My change of mind is about the reality of sin and the decision to turn to God instead. A man doesn't call something crooked unless he has some idea of a straight line. St. John 3:16 states, *"For God so loved the world that He gave His only begotten Son that whosoever believeth in Him should not perish, but have everlasting life."* Today, I have life. The best time of my life is serving God. My wife and I are working together to win souls for the kingdom of God.

Jesus is speaking to his disciples in St. Luke 5:4, *"Now when He had left speaking He said unto Simon, launch out into the deep and let down your nets for a draught."* I believe we must go beyond the four walls of our local church and venture out into areas where there is truly a need. Whether we visit the hospital or nursing homes, the mall, walk around the neighborhood, or even talk to our unsaved loved ones, we must launch out in this time and season and spread the "Good News" of Jesus Christ because time is winding up and Jesus is on His way back for His church. The first message that I preached was not in a church or building. It was in my home with my wife, son, and grandchildren entitled, "The Perfect Storm" and it is one that I will never forget. In the midst of the chaos that was happening in our lives plus the fact that our son and grandchildren were living with us at the time it was truly an experience. This was the first time that anyone had ever lived with us. It just seemed so odd that in the middle, there was a peace that I could not explain. God was blessing us in ways that were unbelievable, and this helped to build our faith and trust God even more through the process. My wife and I would get up on Sunday morning and drive forty-five minutes (one way) to pick up our son and his family for a church service that started at 10:00 a.m. and be on time. As I reflect back on my life, I believe it was a test. How far will you go not just for your family, but for souls? It was perfect because God was in it, and we yielded our will to Him. Christ can make us overcomers by dwelling within us and with His mighty power destroy the power of sin. As you gaze upon Him you will be changed from the inside out. A man may cry for twenty years without the Spirit of the Lord and the more he cries, the fewer people notice him but if he is filled with the Holy Spirit and cries once, people feel the effects. My desire is to cry and be heard. Only one thing will meet the needs of the people and that is for you to be immersed in the life of Jesus Christ. The reason the world is not seeing Jesus is that Christian people are not filled with Jesus. If God lays hold of you by the Spirit, you will find that there is an end to everything and a beginning of God. Your whole body will become seasoned with the divine likeness of God.

The man who lives in the Spirit lives a life of freedom and joy, blessings and service, and a life that brings blessings to others.

About the Author

Dr. Clyde William Floyd was raised at Emmanuel Pentecostal Church of God under the leadership his pastor and mentor, the late Bishop Joseph P. Cooper Sr. Dr. Floyd accepted Jesus Christ as his personal Savior as a young teen and he is currently still an active

As a young man, he strayed away from God however, the Lord spared his life and Dr. Floyd rededicated his life to Christ in November 1991.

Dr. Floyd has been married to his wife, Wanda, for 37 years. They have one son and two grandchildren.

In August of 2001 Dr. Floyd was ordained as a deacon. He currently serves as the Sunday School Superintendent and also teaches the Adult Sunday School class. In June 2014, He was called into the ministry.

In 2019 Dr. Floyd attended the Christian World College of Theology where he pursued dual degrees: a Master's degree in Ministry (Theology) graduating Summa Cum Laude in 2021, and the Newburgh Theological Seminary with a Doctorate of Philosophy in Christian Counseling with a Specialization in Addiction Counseling in 2022.

In March 2020, he retired from Baltimore Air Coil (as a welder) with 25 years of service.

Dr. Floyd's desire is that souls will be saved, set free, and delivered by the power of God.

Wanda Floyd graduated from Dover High School, Dover, Del. in 1974 and attended Morgan State University in Baltimore, Md. for two years.

Mrs. Floyd accepted Jesus Christ as her personal savior in 1990 at Community Pentecostal Church, Inc., Houston, Del. under the leadership of the late Bishop John Cooper. She is currently a member of Emmanuel Pentecostal Church of God Inc., Camden, Del. under the leadership of Pastor Joseph P. Cooper, Jr.

Mrs. Floyd has been married to Dr. Clyde W. Floyd for 37 years. Together they have one son and two grandchildren.

She retired from the State of Delaware as a Food Service Manager after 31 years of service.

Mrs. Floyd's message to those that feel like there is no hope is to try Jesus. He can turn your situation around and make what seems to be impossible possible, if you only believe.

Trailblazers

Bishop Joseph P. Cooper, Sr. and his Sister-in-law, Pastor Emeritus Lula M. Cooper, "sharing a moment!"

Acknowledgements

To my Lord and Savior Jesus Christ for giving me the grace and joy to complete this book. My prayer is that reading it will encourage you through your journey.

Pastor Joseph P. Cooper Jr. (my pastor)- Emmanuel Pentecostal Church of God Inc.

Bishop Marion L. Hendricks (mentor)– Pentecostal Church of God of Lincoln, Inc.

Pastor Joniqua Combs– Community Pentecostal Church of God, Inc.

Pastor Calvin Wilson – Existence Pentecostal Church of God Inc.

Pastor Willie Davis III – Abundant Harvest Ministries, Inc.

Pastor Jamaal Cubbage – Living Vision Holy Church International

Special thanks to – Chancellor Anita Woods, Christian World College of Theology for your support and encouragement throughout this process.

Contact The Author

Email: cwfloyd1958@gmail.com

Facebook: Clyde Floyd

Terry Neal

Owner/Photographer

Bring The Noise Photography

6 Park AVE

Milford, DE 19963

Facebook.com/btn_photos

www.bringthenoisephotography.com

www.grace4purposeco.com

www.ingramcontent.com/pod-product-compliance
Lightning Source LLC
Chambersburg PA
CBRC090824100426
42812CB00020B/2666